English Conversation Lesson Plans (Intermediate-Advanced):

ESL Vocabulary, Idioms, Discussion Questions & Writing Prompts

**Jackie Bolen**

**www.eslactivity.org**

# Table of Contents

# About the Author: Jackie Bolen

I taught English in South Korea for a decade to every level and type of student and I've taught every age from kindergarten kids to adults. Most of my time centered around teaching at two universities: five years at a science and engineering school out in the rice paddies of Chungcheongnam-Do, and four years at a major university in Busan where I taught high-level classes for students majoring in English. These days, I live in Vancouver, Canada where I teach privately as well as in English language academies. In my spare time, you can usually find me outside surfing, biking, hiking, or on the hunt for the most delicious kimchi I can find.

In case you were wondering what my academic qualifications are, I hold a Master of Arts in Psychology. During my time in Korea, I've successfully completed both the Cambridge CELTA and DELTA certification programs. With the combination of almost 15 years teaching ESL/EFL learners of all ages and levels, and the more formal teaching qualifications I've obtained, I have a solid foundation on which to offer teaching advice.

## Jackie Bolen around the Internet

ESL Speaking (www.eslspeaking.org)

YouTube (www.youtube.com/c/jackiebolen)

Pinterest (www.pinterest.ca/eslspeaking)

Facebook (www.facebook.com/eslspeaking)

Email: jb.business.online@gmail.com

Get even more things ESL teaching, delivered straight to your inbox: (www.eslspeaking.org/subscribe).

# How to Use this Book

These conversation lessons are designed for teenagers, university students, or adults. They do assume a basic knowledge of English grammar and vocabulary so are best suited for intermediate or advanced students.

The main purpose of these lessons is to get students talking about a certain topic and can be used for classes of 30 minutes to two hours. Each lesson includes the following:

- warm-up question

- vocabulary challenge (5 scrambled words from the conversation questions)

- idioms and phrases related to the topic (5)

- 10 conversation questions

- 2 writing prompts suitable for class time or homework

For smaller classes of less than three students, it's possible to work through each lesson together as a class. It's also possible to use these conversation lessons for 1-1 or private tutoring. However, for larger classes of four or more, I recommend putting students into pairs and letting them work through the lesson together to make classes more student-centered.

# Artificial Intelligence

## Warm-Up

What comes to mind when you hear the term, "artificial intelligence?"

## Vocabulary Challenge

1. s d i e c v e – things made for a particular purpose

2. o r o b s t – machines that can replicate certain human movements

3. g i t n i t e l n l e – similar to clever, bright, brilliant

4. y r i e s b p l s o n – in a sensible manner

5. t p r i e n d o i c – a guess about the future

## Idioms and Phrases

pushing the envelope, digital footprint, disruptive technology, cutting edge, tech-savvy

1. That new AI program is _____ in terms of what it can do.

2. I'm nervous about _____ too far. You know Keith is reluctant to change.

3. Please slow down. You know I'm not _____.

4. Be careful what you post online. You don't want a harmful _____.

5. In my opinion, the internet is by far the most important _____ of my lifetime.

## Answers

**Vocab**: devices, robots, intelligent, responsibly, prediction

**Idioms**: cutting edge, pushing the envelope, tech-savvy, digital footprint, disruptive technology

**Let's Talk!**

1. What is artificial intelligence (AI)? Look up the definition if you don't know it.

2. What are some examples of AI that people might encounter in their daily lives.

3. Name some ways in which AI can help people.

4. What are some of the dangers of AI?

5. Do you think that AI might be more intelligent than humans one day? Or, is it already?

6. Is there a difference between robots and AI?

7. Will people one day have devices planted inside their bodies that use AI?

8. What's your prediction for what AI will look like in 100 years from now?

9. Can AI ever take over the world?

10. How can we make sure AI is used responsibly?

**Writing Prompts**

1. Do you think that the benefits of AI outweigh the negatives?

2. What steps can be taken to ensure that AI doesn't take over the world in a negative way?

# Consumerism

## Warm-Up

Do you like to go shopping? Why or why not?

## Vocabulary Challenge

1. o f a r c s t – facts or circumstances

2. t f l r u i g y a – the quality of being thrifty

3. m e o c y o n – production and consumption of goods in a society

4. b d t e – something, usually money, that is owed

5. y e l t a h l i c – in a way that relates to moral standards

## Idioms and Phrases

Black Friday, bargain hunting, shopping spree, shop till you drop, window shopping

1. Let's go to the mall. You can _____.

2. I like to buy electronics on _____ usually.

3. I'll go to the mall with you, but I'm only _____. I have no money.

4. My dad is famous for _____. He spends months finding deals.

5. I just got my work bonus. Let's go on a _____!

## Answers

**Vocab**: factors, frugality, economy, debt, ethically

**Idioms**: shop till you drop, Black Friday, window shopping, bargain hunting, shopping spree

**Let's Talk!**

1. What factors influence your decision to buy something?

2. What do you think about frugality?

3. What kind of jobs depend on people buying things?

4. Do you think holidays like Christmas and Easter have lost their original meaning and become too consumeristic?

5. Does the economy of your country depend on people buying things?

6. Would you ever go into debt to buy a consumer product like a TV?

7. Is consumerism hard on the environment?

8. Can people consume ethically? What does this mean?

9. Should companies be allowed to advertise to children?

10. What do companies do to build brand loyalty?


**Writing Prompts**

1. Consumerism is harming our world. Do you agree or disagree with this? Give reasons and examples.

2. What are some ways that people can consume responsibly?

# Customs and Traditions

**Warm-Up**

What are some customs and traditions that people in your country follow with regard to food and eating?

**Vocabulary Challenge**

1. c d i t r e – a straightforward or honest manner

2. s g t n r e a – unusual

3. i e n c d t i r – not in a straightforward manner

4. i w e n d g d – marriage ceremony

5. e r l u  e b k r e r a (2 words) – describes someone who doesn't follow the usual customs or traditions.

**Idioms and Phrases**

that's how we roll, you can't judge a book by its cover, throw caution to the wind, when in Rome, as American as apple pie

1. You know what they say, "_____." You just have to do it.

2. Get used to it! _____ here at ABC company.

3. _____ and ask her out! I think she'll say yes.

4. It looked terrible but tasted good. _____.

5. She is _____. I love the way she talks and acts!

**Answers**

**Vocab**: direct, strange, indirect, wedding, rule breaker

**Idioms**: when in Rome, that's how we roll, throw caution to the wind, you can't judge a book by its cover, as American as apple pie

**Let's Talk!**

1. Is tradition important to you?

2. What's the difference between a custom and a tradition? Look it up if you don't know!

3. What traditions or customs did your family have related to holidays when you were growing up? Do you still do them today?

4. How do people talk to each other in your country? In a direct or indirect manner? What do you think about this?

5. Is it important to follow the customs and traditions of a country you are visiting?

6. Are there customs that visitors to your country might think are strange?

7. What are some wedding traditions that people follow in your country?

8. What are some customs and traditions for birthdays in your country?

9. Do you know anyone who doesn't follow the usual customs or traditions in your country? What do you think about him or her?

10. Are you a rule follower or a rule breaker?


**Writing Prompts**

1. Customs and traditions in a culture should always be respected. Do you agree or disagree with this?

2. Choose a popular holiday in your country. Write about some of the traditions and customs related to it.

# Current Events

## Warm-Up

Where do you find out about the news?

## Vocabulary Challenge

1. s p i o l c i t – activities associated with running a country

2. a c g y e n – an organization that provides a particular service

3. n s e e w r s p a p – written publications about the news

4. a i c m t p – effect on something

5. y t s a e x r p a – people who pay taxes to the government

## Idioms and Phrases

heard through the grapevine, out of the loop, hot off the press, drop a bombshell, go viral

1. How did you know about that already? I just heard. It's _____.

2. We need one of our campaigns to _____.

3. I _____ that Tom is going to get fired.

4. I'm a bit _____. What's happening with that account?

5. Politicians love to _____ on Friday nights when all the reporters are done for the week.

## Answers

**Vocab**: politics, agency, newspapers, impact, taxpayers

**Idioms**: hot off the press, go viral, heard through the grapevine, out of the loop, drop a bombshell

**Let's Talk!**

1. Are you interested in current events and the news?

2. What kinds of news do you most prefer reading about—sports, politics, culture, etc.?

3. How do you know if something you see is fake news?

4. How reliable is news that you see on social media?

5. What stories are in the news these days in your country?

6. Are you following anything in the news from around the world?

7. Does your government have a news agency (for example, the CBC in Canada)? How much do you trust their reporting?

8. Do you ever read or listen to the news in English?

9. Do current events have any impact on your daily life?

10. Are newspapers a dying industry?

**Writing Prompts**

1. The most reliable sources of news come from average citizens reporting things on social media. Do you agree or disagree?

2. My country should have a news agency funded by the taxpayers. Do you agree or disagree with this?

# Dating and Marriage

## Warm-Up

How do most people find someone to date or marry in your country?

## Vocabulary Challenge

1. c r t o m i a n – describes a chosen relationship based on love

2. r d c d i e v o – no longer married

3. a m a e t m r c s k h – people who arrange marriages or romantic relationships

4. g a d r e r e a n  a m a g r e r i (2 words) – a relationship planned by family or a matchmaker, instead of the two people involved.

5. g l a e l – allowable by law

## Idioms and Phrases

tie the knot, shotgun wedding, pop the question, marriage of convenience, cold feet

1. So when is Keith finally going to _____?

2. Amy and Sandy are going to _____ this August.

3. Do you think that Bob is going to get ____? I can't believe he'll really get married!

4. That was so fast. Was it a _____?

5. I wouldn't be opposed to a _____ as long as it benefits both of us.

## Answers

**Vocab**: romantic, divorced, matchmakers, arranged marriage, legal

**Idioms**: pop the question, tie the knot, cold feet, shotgun wedding, marriage of convenience

**Let's Talk!**

1. What is the secret to a happy romantic relationship?

2. Do people place too much value on being in a relationship?

3. How long should people date each other before getting married?

4. Should it be more difficult in your country to get a divorce?

5. Should people live together before getting married?

6. Is gay marriage legal in your country? If it's not, do you think that it should be?

7. What do you think about matchmakers or arranged marriages? Would you ever consider doing this?

8. Why are fewer and fewer people getting married these days?

9. Some people stay married even if they're unhappy because they have kids. What do you think about this?

10. Who is marriage usually better for—men or women?


**Writing Prompts**

1. People shouldn't get divorced except in situations like abuse. Do you agree or disagree?

2. Marriage is an outdated institution. It's better to just live together without getting married. Do you agree or disagree?

# Education

**Warm-Up**

How important do you think education is?

**Vocabulary Challenge**

1. n o n i e l – something done using the internet.

2. s m i e m e o r – something remembered from the past.

3. i t e n s v – spend money on

4. e p a t r i e v – not public

5. o t u n i t i – money paid to attend school, usually a university or college.

**Idioms and Phrases**

pull an all-nighter, hit the books, pass with flying colors, teacher's pet, cut class

1. Sorry, I can't hang out tomorrow. I have to _____.

2. Keith is the _____. It's so annoying.

3. Let's _____. We have a sub. We're not doing anything important.

4. Did you ever _____ when you were in university?

5. You'll _____! No need to worry at all.

**Answers**

**Vocab**: online, memories, invest, private, tuition

**Idioms**: hit the books, teacher's pet, cut class, pull an all-nighter, pass with flying colors

**Let's Talk!**

1. Do you think that you received a good education?

2. What are some of your favorite memories from your school days?

3. What do you think of online education?

4. Should children "fail" a class or do a grade over again? Why or why not?

5. Does your country invest enough money into the education system?

6. What happens if a country doesn't have a good education system?

7. At what age should children start taking tests in school?

8. Should children spend time taking art, music, and gym? Or, focus on things like science and math?

9. What do you think about private schools? Are they common in your country?

10. In some countries, university tuition is free. What do you think about this?

**Writing Prompts**

1. What would you like to change about the education system in your country?

2. Parents and schools are of equal importance for educating children. Do you agree or disagree with this?

# Electronics

## Warm-Up

How addicted are you to your phone? What do you like doing on it?

## Vocabulary Challenge

1. t g e a s d g – small electronic devices

2. s a o l c i   i m e a d (2 words) – Facebook, Instagram, and X are examples of this

3. d s l r i v e e s r   c a s r (2 words) – vehicles that are controlled by computers, not people

4. m l i f i e t e – from birth to death

5. i f o s l s   f l u s e – coal, oil, and gas are examples of this

## Idioms and Phrases

pull the plug, blow a fuse, on the same wavelength, ahead of the curve, all the bells and whistles

1. That was easy. Pizza it is! I think we're _____.

2. I'm going to need to _____ on that new product. It's too difficult to manufacture.

3. Wow! Your new car really has _____.

4. Sandra is going to _____. Watch out.

5. I want to be _____. The first one to market will have all the brand loyalty.

## Answers

**Vocab**: gadgets, social media, driverless cars, lifetime, fossil fuels

**Idioms**: on the same wavelength, pull the plug, all the bells and whistles, blow a fuse, ahead of the curve

**Let's Talk!**

1. Are you someone who likes to have all the latest electronic "gadgets?"

2. Which electronic devices could you not live without?

3. What are some of the negative effects of too much time on electronics?

4. At what age should children be allowed to have a phone?

5. Do you think phones should be allowed in schools?

6. Do you think social media does more harm than good?

7. Will driverless cars be common in your lifetime? What about flying scooters or cars?

8. Do you think that AI will one day take over the world?

9. What will happen to all of our electronics when we run out of fossil fuels?

10. Overal, has technology improved your life, or harmed it?


**Writing Prompts**

1. Young children should be allowed to use electronics. It's just a fact of life these days. Do you agree or disagree?

2. Technology has improved our quality of life, compared to 100 years ago. Do you agree or disagree with this statement?

# Food

## Warm-Up

What's your favorite food? Is there anything you don't like?

## Vocabulary Challenge

1. j k u n   o f d o   i j u e n k (3 words) – someone who eats a lot of unhealthy food

2. v a e n g – describes someone who doesn't eat any animal products

3. i c u e n i s – examples are Chinese, French, Italian, etc.

4. t s e u p n p s l e m – something designed to add nutrition to a diet

5. f d a – short-lived excitement about something

## Idioms and Phrases

eats like a horse, bring home the bacon, like two peas in a pod, go bananas, a piece of cake

1. Don't worry! That test is _____.

2. Sarah and Lucy are _____. I can't even tell them apart from each other.

3. Cook more food! Timmy is bringing his friend John over, and he _____.

4. I need to get a second job and _____. Tom has started playing hockey, and it's very expensive.

5. Let's let the kids _____ for a few minutes now. Then they'll be tired at bedtime.

## Answers

**Vocab**: junk food junkie, vegan, cuisine, supplements, fad

**Idioms**: a piece of cake, like two peas in a pod, eats like a horse, bring home the bacon, go bananas

**Let's Talk!**

1. Do you generally have a healthy or unhealthy diet?

2. Do you know anyone who is a "junk food junkie?"

3. Besides the cuisine of your own country, what other kinds of food do you enjoy?

4. How often do you eat out?

5. Do you "live to eat," or, "eat to live?"

6. What do you think about "fad diets?"

7. Who should we trust for information about nutrition?

8. Would you ever consider becoming vegan?

9. Do you think nutritional supplements and vitamins are helpful or a waste of money?

10. People have strong associations (comfort, stress relief, etc.) with certain foods. Why do you think this is the case?


**Writing Prompts**

1. Children should be taught about healthy eating and cooking in school. Do you agree or disagree with this?

2. Eating less meat has the potential to change the world for the better. What do you think about this statement?

# Friends and Family

## Warm-Up

Who do you spend the most time with—friends or family?

## Vocabulary Challenge

1. e n r u a c l    l f a y m i (2 words) – a couple and their children

2. c b k l a    e s p h e (2 words) – someone who people think brings shame to their family

3. i t n w – 2 children born at the same time from the same person

4. l r e s i p o n t s i y b i — having control over someone

5. u c u r l e t – a way of life shared by a group of people

## Idioms and Phrases

blood is thicker than water, spitting image, father figure, runs in the family, follow in his footsteps

1. Wow! Ted is the _____ of his dad.

2. Bob is a doctor? Is Kevin going to _____?

3. Don't even try to come between those two. _____.

4. Sam was a great _____ for Jeb when he was growing up.

5. Cancer _____. Make sure you get regular screenings.

## Answers

**Vocab**: nuclear family, black sheep, twin, responsibility, culture

**Idioms**: spitting image, follow in his footsteps, blood is thicker than water, father figure, runs in the family

**Let's Talk!**

1. How important are your friends to you?

2. What comes to mind when you hear the word "family?"

3. Should the definition of "family" be expanded beyond the nuclear family?

4. Do you know anyone who no longer speaks to one of their family members? What do you think about that?

5. Does your family have a "black sheep?"

6. Do you have a "family tree?" How far back does it go?

7. Does the oldest child have a lot of responsibility in your culture?

8. Would you like to be a twin? Why or why not?

9. What role did your grandparents have in your life?

10. Who should take care of older people—family or the government?


**Writing Prompts**

1. Our definition of "family" is often too narrow—it should include neighbors, friends, etc. Do you agree or disagree with this?

2. Family above all else. Do you agree with this statement?

# The Future

## Warm-Up

Are you optimistic or pessimistic about the future?

## Vocabulary Challenge

1. a g l o l b   i w a n r g m (2 words) – a rise in the Earth's temperature

2. n i t n o n i o s v a – inventions

3. n f o e r t u   e t s e l r l – people who claim to know the future

4. e p l t a n — Earth, Venus, and Jupiter are examples

5. i p r e o p s h e c – predictions about the future

## Idioms and Phrases

the end times, time will tell, days are numbered, tomorrow is a new day, rain check

1. Don't worry about it. _____.

2. _____ if I studied enough. I won't get my results back for a month.

3. Can I take a _____ on dinner? I'm busy this weekend.

4. Are we in _____? All these natural disasters!

5. His _____. He might only have another week or two.

## Answers

**Vocab**: global warming, innovations, fortune tellers, planet, prophecies

**Idioms**: tomorrow is a new day, time will tell, rain check, the end times, days are numbered

**Let's Talk!**

1.  Do you feel hopeful about the future? Why or why not?

2.  Will global warming make the Earth uninhabitable?

3.  What new innovations will we see in the next 50 years?

4.  Will AI do more harm than good?

5.  Do you remember the days before the internet? What was that like? Or, imagine what it was like if you can't!

6.  Do you think fortune tellers can predict the future?

7.  What are some of your future plans?

8.  Do you think people will ever live on another planet?

9.  What do you think about religious prophecies and predictions?

10. What do you think education will be like in the future?

**Writing Prompts**

1.  Drastic action is needed today to prevent more global warming. Do you agree or disagree?

2.  What current technology will have the biggest impact on our world in 20 years from now?

# Gender Roles

## Warm-Up

What was life at your house like growing up? Did your parents stick to specific chores or gender roles?

## Vocabulary Challenge

i s f p c i e c — not general

t e t x a p o e i c n — a belief that someone will do something

i t a y c p l — normal or usual

a m t a r n o y d — required or obligatory

f s u g c n o i n — not clear

## Idioms and Phrases

glass ceiling, stay home, military service, first dates, gender fluid

That was one of the best _____ that I've ever been on.

After I had a child, the expectation was that I'd _____ to care for him.

I'm thinking about changing jobs because my current company has a serious _____.

_____ means not strictly identifying as either male or female.

In South Korea, males generally have to do two years of _____ in their 20's.

## Answers

**Vocab:** specific, expectation, typical, mandatory, confusing

**Idioms:** first dates, stay home, glass ceiling, gender fluid, military service

# Let's Talk!

1. Do you think there are some jobs that men are better at than women?

2. Are there some jobs that women are better at?

3. Are there specific expectations of men and women in your country?

4. Have you ever heard of the "glass ceiling"? Is this a problem in your country?

5. Do you see yourself as a "typical" man or woman?

6. Do you have children? Who is mostly responsible for caring for them?

7. A man and woman are married, but the woman makes more money at her job. Should the man stay home to care for the children?

8. Are there different expectations for boys and girls growing up in your country?

9. Is there a mandatory military service in your country? Is it equal for both genders?

10. Who should pay for a first date?


## Writing Prompts

1. Men are better at some jobs than women (and vice-versa). Do you agree or disagree?

2. Do you think there is gender equality in your country? Why or why not?

# Going Out to Eat

## Warm-Up

When you eat out, what's your motivation? (Don't like doing dishes, not enough time, it's delicious, etc.)

## Vocabulary Challenge

u r e r n s a t a t — a place to eat a meal outside the home

n i e n d t d e n p e — not part of a chain or a big company

s e v x i p e e n — not cheap

e p g n e t r a c e — %

p t i n i p g — the practice of giving extra money to a server, someone who cuts your hair, a taxi driver, etc.

## Idioms and Phrases

eating out, chain restaurant, chew the fat, too expensive, cup of tea

I'm not _____ these days since I'm saving money to buy a new car.

That restaurant is really good, but I think it's far _____.

My coworker loves to _____, so it's hard to get work done when he's around.

Everyone loves that new band, but they're not my _____.

McDonalds is an example of a _____.

## Answers

**Vocabulary challenge:** restaurant, independant, expensive, percentage, tipping

**Idioms and phrases:** eating out, too expensive, chew the fat, cup of tea, chain restaurant

# Let's Talk!

1. How often do you eat out? What's your favorite restaurant?

2. Where do you go for a cheap, quick meal?

3. What do you think about fast-food restaurants?

4. What are some ways that fast-food restaurants market to kids?

5. Do you prefer chain restaurants or independent ones?

6. Is tipping at restaurants common where you're from? What percentage do you usually tip?

7. If there's a hair in your food, what do you do?

8. If you asked for a steak cooked medium-rare and it's well done, what would you do?

9. Does your family like to eat out to celebrate special occasions like a birthday?

10. Is there a certain kind of restaurant that you wish were closer to your house?


# Writing Prompts

1. Write about one of your favorite restaurants.

2. Describe some of the restaurants around your school or workplace.

# Habits

**Warm-Up**

What are some things that you do every single day?

**Vocabulary Challenge**

1. i m n o g r n   i r o e n u t – a set of habits that someone does after waking up

2. s f u c u c e s l s – having achieved something

3. i s m n o g k – using cigarretes

4. l z a y – opposite of hard worker

5. v a t d i d i e c – describes something that is difficult to stop doing or using

**Idioms and Phrases**

old habits die hard, creature of habit, an apple a day keeps the doctor away, get in the habit, quit cold turkey

1. You know Mary. She's a _____ and goes to bed at 10:30 every night.

2. I want to _____ of taking my lunch to work.

3. Smoking? Not any more! I _____.

4. It'll take a while to quit. _____.

5. My doctor told me that _____! She was saying that I need to eat healthier.

**Answers**

**Vocab**: morning routine, successful, smoking, lazy, addictive

**Idioms**: creature of habit, get in the habit, quit cold turkey, old habits die hard, an apple a day keeps the doctor away

## Let's Talk!

1. What are some of your good habits?

2. What are some of your bad habits?

3. Some people have a "morning routine." What do you think about that?

4. Do you find it easy to build a new habit into your life?

5. What are some habits that successful people have?

6. What are some habits that would help you learn English?

7. Have you broken any bad habits like smoking?

8. What advice would you give to someone who was really lazy?

9. Smoking is very addictive and is a hard habit to break. Should companies be required to make cigarettes less addictive?

10. Do any of your family members have habits that annoy you?


## Writing Prompts

1. Write about a time that you tried to break a bad habit or start a new, good one.

2. People with too many habits are inflexible and leave no room for fun in their lives. Do you agree or disagree with this?

# Holidays

## Warm-Up

What was your favourite holiday growing up?

## Vocabulary Challenge

1. n t i r a d o s i t – how beliefs are passed from generation to generation

2. c p l u i b – not private

3. a p d a e r – a public walk with bands, floats, etc.

4. i c o d m z m e r c e i a l – designed mainly for financial gain

5. a f e s l t i s v – days or periods of celebration

## Idioms and Phrases

white Christmas, ring in the New Year, holiday spirit, stuffed, pull all your eggs in one basket

1. How are you going to _____?

2. I'm _____. I can't eat another bite!

3. Do you think we'll have a _____ this year?

4. Have another drink. It'll help you get into the _____.

5. Are you sure? I don't think it's wise to _____.

## Answers

**Vocab**: traditions, public, parade, commercialized, festivals

**Idioms**: ring in the New Year, stuffed, white Christmas, holiday spirit, put all your eggs in one basket

**Let's Talk!**

1. What kinds of food do people in your country eat during big holidays?

2. What are some holiday traditions that your family has?

3. Are there enough public holidays in your country (days off of work)?

4. Do you think some holidays are too commercialized?

5. Are there any holidays that are overrated?

6. Would you prefer to spend holidays with family or friends?

7. On which holidays do people give gifts or money in your country?

8. Do you know of any differences in how a holiday is celebrated in your country, compared to another country?

9. Are there any new public holidays in your country? What do you think about them?

10. Do you like parades or festivals with lots of people?


**Writing Prompts**

1. Choose one of the most popular holidays in your country. Describe it to someone who doesn't know anything about it.

2. Religious holidays like Christmas and Easter are too commercialized. Do you agree or disagree?

# Cooking at Home

**Warm-Up**

Do you enjoy cooking at home?

**Vocabulary Challenge**

f b r a e s a k t — the first meal of the day

e m a l —breakfast, lunch, or dinner

g v e n a — someone who doesn't eat any animal products

u y l n t h e a — describes something harmful to the body

i i n e v t — to ask someone to do something with you

**Idioms and Phrases**

eat out, take out, dietary restrictions, kitchen appliances, cooking with gas

I want to save some money, so I need to stop ordering _____ all the time.

This weekend, my family is going shopping for some new _____ like a blender and a toaster.

The new procedures mean that we're _____ now at my company.

My family likes to _____ for birthdays.

My brother has a ton of _____, so it's difficult to cook for him.

**Answers**

**Vocab:** breakfast, meal, vegan, unhealthy, invite

**Idioms:** take out, kitchen appliances, cooking with gas, eat out, dietary restrictions

# Let's Talk!

1. In one week, how often do you eat out?

2. Would you consider yourself to be a good cook?

3. What are some of the meals you regularly make?

4. Do you like cooking with meat? Are you a vegan, or have any other dietary restrictions?

5. Do you have any favorite kitchen appliances?

6. Do you do anything special for weekend breakfasts?

7. What are some special things you cook if someone is coming over for dinner?

8. Do you enjoy cooking a big holiday or family meal, or do you find it stressful?

9. What are some of the first things you learned how to cook when you were a kid?

10. What do you think about meal prep boxes where you get all the ingredients and a recipe but have to cook it yourself? Are they popular where you live?

## Writing Prompts

1. Describe some of the meals that you regularly eat at home.

2. How did you learn to cook?

# Natural Disasters

## Warm-Up

Name at least five natural disasters. Which ones can happen in your country?

## Vocabulary Challenge

1. e m e c e r i g e s n – big, urgent problems

2. t c a l e i m   c g h e a n (2 words) – the average temperature of the Earth increasing

3. t i e r s r m o r – the use of violence against regular citizens

4. o a s i t e d r – a small rock that orbits the sun which can sometimes hit the Earth

5. e m a i t i t g – make less severe or serious

## Idioms and Phrases

calm before the storm, weather the storm, a recipe for disaster, stealing my thunder, a walking disaster

1. Hang in there. You'll be able to _____.

2. Oh you know Bob. He's famous for _____ on projects.

3. Enjoy it! These months are the _____ that is law school.

4. Sammy is _____. I wouldn't even trust him to water my plants.

5. Those nails sticking out are _____.

## Answers

**Vocab**: emergencies, climate change, terrorism, asteroid, mitigate

**Idioms**: weather the storm, stealing my thunder, calm before the storm, a walking disaster, a recipe for disaster

**Let's Talk!**

1. Have you ever lived through a natural disaster?

2. Do you have a "disaster kit" at your house?

3. How can we be prepared for emergencies?

4. Are natural disasters happening more frequently because of climate change?

5. Should we be more concerned about terrorism or natural disasters?

6. Do you worry about an asteroid hitting Earth?

7. Why do you think poor people are most impacted by natural disasters?

8. What's a good natural disaster movie that you've seen? Why do you think they're so popular?

9. What's the difference between a hurricane, typhoon, and cyclone?

10. Can technology help mitigate the damage caused by natural disasters?

**Writing Prompts**

1. Who is responsible for preparing for natural disasters—people or governments? Give reasons for your opinion.

2. Are there any positives that can come out of a natural disaster?

# The Environment

## Warm-Up

What things do you do to care for the environment?

## Vocabulary Challenge

1. e t n v e i r n o n m – the natural world

2. s r e r v e e – go back or change direction

3. y t o e c g h n o l – the application of science for practical purposes

4. s r d i t s e a – a sudden, negative event

5. m n u l a t i n l a t i o – a company that operates in many countries

## Idioms and Phrases

a drop in the ocean, hot potato, voice in the wilderness, time is running out, tip of the iceberg

1. The president never talks about that _____.

2. _____ for us to reverse climate change.

3. Asking people to recycle is _____ compared to what actually needs to be done.

4. David Suzuki was a _____ for decades about climate change.

5. The natural disasters we're experiencing now are only the _____.

## Answers

**Vocab**: environment, reverse, technology, disaster, multinational

**Idioms**: hot potato, time is running out, a drop in the ocean, voice in the wilderness, tip of the iceberg

**Let's Talk!**

1. Do you worry about global warming?

2. Is your government doing enough to protect the environment?

3. Will we be able to reverse global warming?

4. Does technology have the potential to save our Earth from environmental disaster?

5. What role does consuming less animal products play in preventing climate change?

6. What do you think of environmental groups like Sea Shepherd and Greenpeace?

7. Are you "environmentally friendly?"

8. Who contributes more to global warming—individuals or big, multinational companies?

9. Do you know what a carbon footprint is? If you don't know, look it up!

10. What role does minimalism play in preventing climate change?


**Writing Prompts**

1. What are some steps that individuals can take to prevent further global warming?

2. Governments around the world need to take immediate action to prevent climate change. Do you agree or disagree with this statement?

# The Legal System

**Warm-Up**

Do you think the legal system is generally effective in your country?

**Vocabulary Challenge**

1. t c o n r i r u o p – dishonest actions by people in power

2. t e l e d c e – someone chosen by voting

3. a e p t p o d i n – someone assigned a role or job

4. n d e d f u – prevent a group from receiving more money

5. d u m n a e r – without a weapon

**Idioms and Phrases**

above board, caught red handed, under the table, cook the books, a slap on the wrist

1. That's so much tax! Can we _____ to avoid some of it?

2. Alex was _____ stealing office supplies.

3. Let's make sure we are _____ on our financial transactions.

4. Let's do this deal _____ and not pay all those fees.

5. White collar criminals usually just get _____.

**Answers**

**Vocab**: corruption, elected, appointed, defund, unarmed

**Idioms**: cook the books, caught red handed, above board, under the table, a slap on the wrist

**Let's Talk!**

1. Is corruption a problem in your country?

2. How much power do the police have in your country?

3. Are judges elected or appointed in your country?

4. What would life look like if there was no legal system?

5. In the USA, there is a push to defund the police. What do you think about this?

6. What should the punishment be for police violence against unarmed citizens?

7. What are some countries that are known for having strict laws and punishments?

8. What are some crimes that you think are easy to get away with?

9. Do the rich and poor get treated differently by legal systems?

10. What are gun laws like in your country?


**Writing Prompts**

1. Guns should be strictly banned for private citizens. Do you agree or disagree with this?

2. What are some ways in which the legal system could be improved in your country?

# Manners

## Warm-Up

Do you have a "pet peeve" related to manners?

## Vocabulary Challenge

1. p i u c b l   t r i a n o s p o r n t a t (2 words) – examples are bus, train, subway

2. i p t o e l – acting in a respectful manner

3. i m n a f o l r – casual

4. r d u e – not polite; disrespectful

5. e n a g t i   o t u (2 words) – having food at a restaurant

## Idioms and Phrases

black tie event, watch your language, speak out of turn, bedside manner, excuse my French

1. Tim! _____. We don't speak like that at our house.

2. I don't want to _____, but I need to point out a glaring oversight.

3. _____, but what the *&^%&&?!?!

4. It's a _____. I'll need to rent or buy something.

5. Dr. Salam has a nice _____. She's so caring.

## Answers

**Vocab**: public transportation, polite, informal, rude, eating out

**Idioms**: watch your language, speak out of turn, excuse my French, black tie event, bedside manner

**Let's Talk!**

1. What are some examples of good and bad manners on public transportation?

2. What are some examples of good and bad manners when eating out?

3. Are people more, or less polite than in the past?

4. At what age should children be taught good manners?

5. Do you know someone who is often quite rude? What are they like?

6. What are some examples of manners in other countries that are different from your country?

7. Do some countries care more about being polite than others?

8. If someone was on a bus watching a movie without earphones, would you say anything to them?

9. What are some situations where you need to be very polite? What are some informal situations?

10. Does your first language have a way to speak more, or less politely?

**Writing Prompts**

1. Children should be taught good manners as soon as possible. Do you agree or disagree with this?

2. What social function do manners serve?

# Modern Life

## Warm-Up

How does modern life compare to life 100 years ago?

## Vocabulary Challenge

1. s c g h a l e l e n – difficulties

2. s l n o e n e l s i – feeling of sadness because of lack of friends

3. t s o y c i e – people living together in a community

4. a s u b e s t l a i n – able to be maintained

5. r l e i s e u – free time

## Idioms and Phrases

rat race, couch potato, keep up with the Joneses, creature comforts, live beyond your means

1. Toby is such a _____. I'm worried about his health.

2. The key to being rich is to not _____.

3. All I want are a few _____. A car, a nice place to live.

4. You know Ted. Doing the _____ thing; always busy working.

5. We're going to go broke trying to _____.

## Answers

**Vocab**: challenges, loneliness, society, sustainable, leisure

**Idioms**: couch potato, live beyond your means, creature comforts, rat race, keep up with the Joneses

**Let's Talk!**

1. What are some adjectives that you'd use to describe modern life?

2. What are some challenges that people face in today's society?

3. How has the internet changed modern life?

4. Do you think loneliness has increased or decreased compared to 100 years ago?

5. Is there too much pressure on the nuclear family these days?

6. Is modern life not sustainable from an environmental perspective?

7. Do you think 40 hours of work per week is a good amount?

8. If you could go back in time and live again, what time period would you go to?

9. What kind of education do people need for modern society?

10. What kinds of leisure activities do you enjoy?


**Writing Prompts**

1. Modern life makes people lonely. Do you agree or disagree with this statement?

2. Four-day work weeks are better for society. Do you agree with this?

# Places Around Your House

## Warm-Up

Would you like to move somewhere else? Or, are you happy with where you live?

## Vocabulary Challenge

1. a f o m s u —something or someone that is widely known

2. e r n s t u t r a a —a place to eat outside the home

3. o c e v e n i t n n — describes something that is easy to access

4. e w k d e n e — Saturday and Sunday

5. e n h r g i o b s — people that live near you

## Idioms and Phrases

public transport, city slicker, concrete jungle, grow up, middle of nowhere

1. My brother is a serious _____. He never wants to go camping or hiking with me.

2. I hated taking _____, so I bought a car.

3. He didn't _____ here, unlike most of the people that live here.

4. That place was in the _____. I had to keep driving and driving!

5. New York is mostly a _____, except for Central Park.

## Answers

**Vocab:** famous, restaurant, convenient, weekend, neighbors

**Idioms:** city slicker, public transport, grow up, middle of nowhere, concrete jungle

46

## Let's Talk!

1. What do you like about where you live? What do you dislike about where you live?

2. What are some reasons that people might move to your neighborhood?

3. Are there any famous areas or sights near where you live?

4. What are some of your favorite restaurants near your house?

5. Can you walk to do shopping or do you have to drive to pick up most things?

6. Do you need a car to get around your town or is the public transport system adequate?

7. What are five adjectives you'd use to describe your neighborhood (busy, quiet, etc.)?

8. Do you know your neighbors? What are they like?

9. What are three things you'd like to do to improve your neighborhood?

10. Did you grow up where you live now? If not, how do they compare?


## Writing Prompts

1. Describe where you live.

2. Compare your neighborhood with another one in your city.

# Places Around the World

## Warm-Up

Is your country known for anything special?

## Vocabulary Challenge

1. d h y o a l i — a special day

2. o f s a u m — something that most people know

3. i a l e l s — describes joining together formally, usually countries

4. a v n a o c i t — when you don't have to go to work or school

5. m s O p l c y i — worldwide sports event

## Idioms and Phrases

world tour, length of time, go Dutch, all Greek to me, strong allies

1. I'm so excited! My favorite band just announced their upcoming _____.

2. The USA and Canada are _____.

3. Learning Mandarin is _____.

4. My boyfriend and I always _____ on dates.

5. I think the ideal _____ for a vacation is around 2 weeks.

## Answers

**Vocab**: holiday, famous, allies, vacation, Olympics

**Idioms**: world tour, strong allies, all Greek to me, go Dutch, length of time

**Let's Talk!**

1. What are 15 ways to describe a country?

2. How would you describe your country?

3. What are the major holidays in your country?

4. Are there any famous foods from your country?

5. Does your country have any strong allies?

6. Is there a country you want to visit in the future?

7. Is there a place you wouldn't want to visit?

8. What's one of the best countries to live in? What is a country that you wouldn't want to live in? Why?

9. Are there some countries that are better than others or are they just different?

10. Do you feel pride in your country during things like the World Cup or the Olympics?

**Writing Prompts**

1. What are some things that you appreciate about your country? What are some things you don't like?

2. What is the best country to live in? Why?

# Religion

**Warm-Up**

What are some of the major world religions?

**Vocabulary Challenge**

1. C h r h u c – a place where Christians meet

2. n e x c i e s t – the state of living

3. i A g n s o s m t i c – belief that it's impossible to know whether or not god exists

4. i p o a l i n t i s c – people who hold public office (usually are elected)

5. e h i r g h   e p r o w (2 words) – god

**Idioms and Phrases**

the Bible belt, act of God, cross to bear, snowball's chance in Hell, the Devil is in the details

1. I have a _____ of passing that test.

2. It's not that bad. Honestly. It's just my _____ in life.

3. That flood is an _____.

4. Please double-check those figures. _____.

5. Why do you want to move to _____?

**Answers**

**Vocab**: Church, existence, Agnosticism, politicians, higher power

**Idioms**: snowball's chance in Hell, cross the bear, act of God, the Devil is in the details, the Bible belt

## Let's Talk!

1. What are the most popular religions in your country?

2. What are some of the positive things about religion?

3. What are some of the negatives?

4. Do you think that all religions are basically the same?

5. In North America and Europe, fewer and fewer people are attending Church. Why do you think this is?

6. Is it possible for people with different religions to live together peacefully?

7. What lessons can we learn from religious leaders like Buddha, Jesus, or Mohammed?

8. Is it possible to prove the existence of some higher power?

9. What do you think about Agnosticism?

10. Religion is a private matter and shouldn't be talked about by people like politicians. Do you agree with this?


## Writing Prompts

1. Religion should be taught in schools. Do you agree or disagree with this statement?

2. What are some of the pros and cons of religion?

# Science

## Warm-Up

Do you stay up-to-date with the latest scientific advancements?

## Vocabulary Challenge

1. s i n i v n e o n t – discoveries

2. c r e r s e h a – study to discover facts

3. s b u s i s n e – dealing with money and commerce

4. a u b t s o e l – total

5. v d i e s c r o – find

## Idioms and Phrases

it's not rocket science, reinvent the wheel, on the same wavelength, once in a blue moon, pull the plug

1. Let's use the code that Ted did last year. We don't need to _____.

2. We're _____ about hiring her.

3. Ethan only cleans his room _____.

4. Doing laundry? _____. I can teach you.

5. We need to _____ on that event. We've only sold 100 tickets.

## Answers

**Vocab**: inventions, research, business, absolute, discover

**Idioms**: reinvent the wheel, on the same wavelength, once in a blue moon, it's not rocket science, pull the plug

**Let's Talk!**

1. Is science important to you?

2. Did you enjoy science in school?

3. What are some of the most important scientific inventions?

4. Do you always trust science?

5. What are some reasons that people might do bad research?

6. What are some reasons that people might not want to study science in schools?

7. When someone says, "It's not rocket science," what does that mean?

8. If you had kids, would you rather have them study science or business? Why?

9. Are there still things left to discover?

10. Can science provide us with absolute truth?


**Writing Prompts**

1. Science can sometimes be dangerous. Do you agree with this statement?

2. Choose one important scientific invention. Describe it, and talk about why it's so important.

# Shopping

## Warm-Up

Do you enjoy shopping?

## Vocabulary Challenge

1. n o n e l i – using the Internet

2. t a d e d i d c – unable to stop doing something

3. c m o n e s r u  u c u r l e t (2 words) – a society centred on buying things

4. r g r o y c e  g s i h o p n p (2 words) – buying food

5. d b r s a n – Toyota, Nike, and Burger King are examples of

## Idioms and Phrases

shop till you drop, bargain hunting, Black Friday, a lemon, costs an arm and a leg

1. Do you enjoy _____ shopping? I usually don't go—I'm so tired from Thanksgiving.

2. Wow! That hotel _____.

3. You love to _____. I don't think I can go with you!

4. I enjoy _____ for anything that costs more than $100.

5. My son bought _____. It has cost him so much money in repairs.

## Answers

**Vocab**: online, addicted, consumer culture, grocery shopping, brands

**Idioms**: Black Friday, costs an arm and a leg, shop till you drop, bargain hunting, a lemon

## Let's Talk!

1. Where do you usually buy clothes?

2. What kinds of things do you buy online?

3. Do you ever shop because you're bored?

4. Do you know anyone who is addicted to shopping?

5. Do you like to compare prices and shop around before buying something?

6. Is our consumer culture destroying the Earth?

7. What are the pros and cons of shopping alone, compared to with other people?

8. Who does the grocery shopping at your house? How often do they go?

9. Are you loyal to any brands? Why?

10. Have you ever been to any night markets? What was that experience like?


## Writing Prompts

1. Write about the last big thing you purchased. How did you make the decision about what to buy?

2. Describe what fast fashion is. Why is it so bad for our world?

# Social Trends

## Warm-Up

Are families getting smaller or larger in your country?

## Vocabulary Challenge

1. i n m t p l i o i c s a – conclusions that can be drawn

2. l h o d u s o e h    d t e b – combined money owing of people in a house

3. i m i m i o g r n a t – moving permanently to a foreign country

4. e c o t n d n e c – joined

5. i r g i n s – increasing

## Idioms and Phrases

fad diet, jump on the bandwagon, cancelled, in the red, quiet quitting

1. We are _____ every single month. One of us needs to get a better job.

2. I don't want to _____, but that toy is really cool!

3. _____ is a good option perhaps? Just do the bare minimum.

4. Have you ever done a _____? Was it effective?

5. That guy is _____. He said some terrible things on social media last week.

## Answers

**Vocab**: implications, household debt, immigration, connected, rising

**Idioms**: in the red, jump on the bandwagon, quiet quitting, fad diet, cancelled

**Let's Talk!**

1. Is the population in your country ageing? If yes, what are some of the implications of this?

2. Are household debt levels rising? Why might this be the case?

3. People are more connected to the Internet. Does this mean that they're less connected to each other?

4. Is immigration changing your country? How?

5. Is religion growing or declining in your country? How does this impact society?

6. Do work and jobs look differently today than 50 years ago?

7. Are people generally healthier, or unhealthier compared to 50 years ago?

8. What is a "fad?" Can you name a few from the past few years?

9. Families are generally getting smaller. What are the pros and cons of this?

10. How has society changed since Covid?


**Writing Prompts**

1. Covid changed our world forever. Do you agree or disagree with this?

2. Choose one social trend happening in your country right now. Why is it important, and what do you think about it?

# Stress

## Warm-Up

What are some things that can cause stress?

## Vocabulary Challenge

1. s t i r e a t e s g – plans of action

2. e r e t g r – a feeling of sadness about some action

3. v r e l e i e – cause something to be less severe

4. i r e n d g u c – making less

5. n s i g s – something that can indicate something else

## Idioms and Phrases

burn the midnight oil, stressed out, bit off more than I can chew, sweating bullets, rack my brain

1. I'm _____ about that test I have to do tomorrow.

2. You're always _____ about your job. Maybe you should find a new one?

3. I have to _____ for a few weeks during tax season.

4. I think I _____ with this project at work.

5. Let me _____. I can't quite remember who has that book.

## Answers

**Vocab**: strategies, regret, relieve, reducing, signs

**Idioms**: sweating bullets, stressed out, burn the midnight oil, bit off more than I can chew, rack my brain

**Let's Talk!**

1. How stressful is your life, on a scale of 1-10? What causes this stress?

2. Are people more "stressed out" today, compared to 50 years ago?

3. What are some signs of stress?

4. What are some strategies for reducing stress?

5. Do you think men or women generally have more stress?

6. What would be more stressful to you—breaking up with someone, or losing your job?

7. Do you find learning English stressful? Why or why not?

8. Technology can make certain things easier (online shopping is one example). Does it also contribute to stress in peoples' lives?

9. Do you like watching the news, or do you find it stressful?

10. Have you ever done something you regret (yelling at someone, breaking something, etc.) because you've been under a lot of stress?

**Writing Prompts**

1. Stress can lead to an early death. Do you agree or disagree with this?

2. Talk about some stressful things in your life, and also some ways that you relieve stress.

# Success and Failure

**Warm-Up**

What are some things that people can succeed or fail at?

**Vocabulary Challenge**

1. e p u r e s r s – stress

2. l c u k – success or failure caused by chance

3. d t e f l a u – the automatic or usual choice

4. s e u s c s c e s – accomplishments

5. e l i f   n l s e o s (2 words) – useful knowledge gained from something

**Idioms and Phrases**

close but no cigar, blow up in my face, take a chance, back to square one, an ace up my sleeve

1. _____ and go on a date with her! I think you'll like her.

2. You're _____. Try again.

3. Don't worry. I have _____ for this negotiation.

4. We're _____ on looking for a place to live. That other deal fell through.

5. I'm scared that this might _____. We don't have enough staff to get it done in time.

**Answers**

**Vocab**: pressure, luck, default, successes, life lesson

**Idioms**: take a chance, close but no cigar, an ace up my sleeve, back to square one, blow up in my face

**Let's Talk!**

1. What are some of your biggest successes in life?

2. What are some of your biggest failures in life?

3. Describe a successful person.

4. Is your idea of success and failure the same as your parents?

5. Is it easier or more difficult to succeed today, compared to 50 years ago?

6. How much pressure should parents put on their children to be successful?

7. Do you think people can generally learn a life lesson from failures?

8. How do you know when you should give up on something?

9. What role does luck play in success?

10. Do you think people can make their own luck?


**Writing Prompts**

1. Money is often the default we use to measure how successful someone is. Do you think this is a good way to measure it? Why or why not?

2. Talk about a failure that you've experienced. What happened, and what did you learn from it?

# Superstitions

## Warm-Up

Do you consider yourself to be a superstitious person?

## Vocabulary Challenge

1. u y n l u k c — not lucky

2. e i e n f n l c u — have an effect on something

3. g t h s o s — dead people reappear as living

4. s a u u l p e r r n a t — some force that can't be explained by science or nature

5. a d m r s e — thoughts that happen when sleeping

## Idioms and Phrases

Friday the 13th, lucky number 7, black cats, knock on wood, bless you

1. Achhoooo! _____.

2. I don't want to move on _____. I think it's a bad sign.

3. Many people don't want to adopt _____ because they think they're bad luck.

4. Let's go with _____! We can't lose.

5. _____, but I think the worst is over.

## Answers

**Vocab**: unlucky, influence, ghosts, supernatural, dreams

**Idioms**: bless you, Friday the 13th, black cats, lucky number 7, knock on wood

**Let's Talk!**

1. What are some popular superstitions in your country?

2. Do you know any superstititions from other countries?

3. Do you believe that some numbers, days, or dates are bad luck?

4. Would you ever change your phone number or move to prevent unlucky numbers?

5. Can you do anything to prevent bad luck?

6. Do you consider yourself to be a lucky person?

7. Do you think that the time and date of your birth have any influence on your life?

8. Do you believe in ghosts or other supernatural things?

9. What do you think happens to someone after they die?

10. Do you think that dreams can tell us things about our lives?


**Writing Prompts**

1. We can make our own "luck" through planning and hard work. Do you agree or disagree with this?

2. Do some research about a popular superstition in your country. What is the history behind it?

# Time

## Warm-Up

How do you spend most of your time?

## Vocabulary Challenge

a e r x t — in addition, also, besides

x r g e n l a i — peaceful; not stressful

c t l y a p i — usual or normal

a m s e s i n g t n — something that you have to do, usually for school

e b o d r — a feeling, the opposite of excited

## Idioms and Phrases

free time, day of the week, school assignments, work project, time is money

I require that my son finishes his _____ before going out to play with his friends.

My favorite _____ is Sunday.

That _____ is probably going to take at least a few months.

My dad always used to say, "_____."

I loved being a student because I always felt like I had lots of _____.

## Answers

**Vocab:** extra, relaxing, typical, assignment, bored

**Idioms:** school assignments, day of the week, work project, time is money, free time

## Let's Talk!

1. What do you like to do in your free time?

2. Do you feel like you have enough free time?

3. What would you do if you had an extra 5 hours each day?

4. What's your busiest day of the week? What's your most relaxing day?

5. Do you usually feel like time moves slowly or quickly?

6. What was the best time in your life so far?

7. Describe your typical day.

8. Are you ever late for things? What usually causes this?

9. Have you ever turned in a school assignment or a work project late?

10. Do you get bored easily?


## Writing Prompts

1. What would you do if you had more time each day?

2. Do you want time to move more slowly or more quickly? Why?

# Travel

## Warm-Up

Talk about the last vacation you took.

## Vocabulary Challenge

1. g p a e c a k   t r o s u (2 words) – a vacation organized by a travel agent

2. c h i a s t l o r i   s e i s t – places of particular importance

3. i t o t s u s r – people who travel for leisure

4. a i d l e – most perfect

5. h b s e a e c – pieces of land along the edge of the water

## Idioms and Phrases

off the beaten track, backseat driver, pack light, budget traveler, hit the road

1. _____. Our baggage allowance is only 10 kg.

2. Let's _____. We need to be there by 7:00.

3. When I travel, I like to go _____, away from all the tourists.

4. Talk to Amy about going to Costa Rica. She's a serious _____. I'm sure she'll have some tips for you.

5. What are some of your favourite _____ for snorkelling?

## Answers

**Vocab**: package tour, historical sites, tourists, ideal, beaches

**Idioms**: pack light, hit the road, off the beaten track, budget traveler, backseat driver

**Let's Talk!**

1. What was the best vacation you've ever taken?

2. Where do you want to go on vacation in the future?

3. Did your family used to go on vacations when you were a kid?

4. What are some things that can go wrong when traveling?

5. Do you prefer planning your own vacation or going on a package tour?

6. What kinds of vacations do you most enjoy—historical sites, shopping trips, beaches, camping, etc.?

7. How much vacation time do you get each year? Is it enough?

8. Do you live in a place where you like to travel to escape bad weather?

9. In your opinion, what's the ideal length of time for a vacation?

10. Do you think you'd like to travel for an entire year?


**Writing Prompts**

1. What places do you recommend tourists visit in your country?

2. What are some of the reasons that people like to travel?

# TV and Movies

**Warm-Up**

How often do you watch TV or movies?

**Vocabulary Challenge**

1. r g e n e — kind of movie or TV show

2. r h o r o r — a scary movie

3. s a c s t e r e s — women who act in movies or TV shows

4. i m o e v   e t h r e t a (2 words) — a place where people watch movies

5. d e o r c u i m e s n t a = a movie or TV show that provides a factual report of something

**Idioms and Phrases**

let's cut, magic hour, that's a wrap, couch potato, rolling

1. _____! Go home and enjoy the weekend.

2. _____. I think we have some good shots.

3. Let's go during _____. We can get some nice pictures of the kids.

4. Time to get _____ if we don't want to be late.

5. I'm worried about my son who is a _____.

**Answers**

**Vocab**: genre, horror, actresses, movie theater, documentaries

**Idioms**: that's a wrap, let's cut, magic hour, rolling, couch potato

**Let's Talk!**

1. What's the last TV show or movie that you watched?

2. What genre of movies or TV shows do you like?

3. Which genre do you not like?

4. Who are some of your favourite actors or actresses?

5. Have you ever watched a movie multiple times?

6. Do you generally think books, or movies based on books are better?

7. Do you like watching horror movies?

8. Do you like going to the movie theater, or do you like watching movies at home?

9. What do you think about documentaries?

10. Do you subscribe to any streaming services like Netflix or Amazon Prime? Are they a good value for you?

**Writing Prompts**

1. TV and movies are a waste of time. Do you agree or disagree with this?

2. TV shows and movies can influence the culture in a positive, or negative way. Do you agree with this statement?

# Weather

## Warm-Up

What kind of weather do you like best? Why?

## Vocabulary Challenge

m s e u r m — the season where you might go to the beach

t w r i n e — the season where you might go skiing

e a v a e g r — central or typical value in a set of numbers

r t e t m p u e e r a — Celcius and Fahrenheit are units of this

a b a l r i z d — a very bad snowstorm

## Idioms and Phrases

raining cats and dogs, extreme weather, got wind of it, on cloud nine, saving for a rainy day

Global warming is a likely reason that we're getting more _____ lately.

I tried to plan a surprise party for my wife but she _____.

My grandparents are always _____.

I'm going to stay inside and read a book because it's _____.

I was _____ after seeing my test score.

## Answers

**Vocab:** summer, winter, average, temperature, blizzard

**Idioms:** extreme weather, got wind of it, saving for a rainy day, raining cats and dogs, on cloud nine

# Let's Talk!

1. What's the weather like in each season in your country?

2. What are some activities that people do in each season?

3. What's your favorite season? Why?

4. What's your least favorite season? Why?

5. Which season is the most beautiful?

6. What kind of weather do you hate?

7. Would you rather live in a place that's always hot or always cold?

8. Do you think we're getting more extreme weather lately because of global warming?

9. Has extreme weather like a tornado, blizzard, or earthquake ever impacted your life?

10. What kind of weather do you prefer when choosing a vacation?

# Writing Prompts

1. Describe your ideal day in terms of weather.

2. Global warming is changing weather patterns in my country. Do you agree or disagree?

# Work and Business

## Warm-Up

Have you had any bad customer service experiences? Talk about 1-2 of them.

## Vocabulary Challenge

o c p y m n a —a business

u c r t e s m o —a person who buys a product or service

b n o i d r o o e h g h —the area around where you live

l s g n o a — a saying

c r s n e o i s e — an economic slump

## Idioms and Phrases

customer service, gig economy, bail out, big picture, get down to business

What a terrible _____ experience! I was on hold for 45 minutes.

I always remember to focus on the _____ instead of getting caught up in the small details.

I disagreed with the big government _____ package for big businesses during Covid-19.

No more chit-chat, let's _____.

One of the disadvantages of the _____ is a lack of benefits and stability for workers.

## Answers

**Vocab:** company, customer, neighborhood, slogan, recession

**Idioms:** customer service, big picture, bail out, get down to business, gig economy

## Let's Talk!

1. Are there any companies that you love to support? Why? Are there any companies that you choose not to support? Why?

2. Do you like to support small businesses?

3. Do you know anyone with their own business? Describe it.

4. What are some advantages and disadvantages of working for yourself?

5. Is the "gig economy" (freelance or contract work) a big thing in your country?

6. Should the government "bail out" big business during a recession? Why or why not?

7. Together, name 5 slogans from companies that you know (Just do it!).

8. Does every business need a website these days?

9. If you could work abroad, would you choose to do it?

10. What are some qualities of a good company CEO or owner?


## Writing Prompts

1. Would you prefer to work for someone else or work for yourself? Why?

2. Describe the ideal boss.

# Work-Life Balance

**Warm-Up**

What is work-life balance? If you don't know, look it up on Google!

**Vocabulary Challenge**

1. l r e i e s u – time not spent working or studying

2. r e y m e p l o – a person or organization that employs people

3. s e m e p e l o y – people who work

4. i p o r o n m s o t – raising to a higher position at work

5. a c o r t p o e r   e l a d r d – the company hierarchy (moving from basic level to the top)

**Idioms and Phrases**

the rat race, burning the midnight oil, all work and no play, pace of life, climbing the corporate ladder

1. I can't sustain this _____. Something has to give.

2. I want to get out of _____ and move to the countryside.

3. I'm sick and tired of _____. I need more sleep.

4. Tim is _____ at a rapid pace! He's already a director.

5. _____ makes Tom a grumpy boy! Why don't you take up a hobby?

**Answers**

**Vocab**: leisure, employer, employees, promotions, corporate ladder

**Idioms**: pace of life, the rat race, burning the midnight oil, climbing the corporate ladder, all work and no play

**Let's Talk!**

1. Why is work-life balance important?

2. Do you think you have a good balance between work and leisure?

3. What are some things that contribute to a bad work-life balance?

4. Are you expected to be available all the time for your job? What do you think about this situation?

5. Do employers have a responsibility to ensure that employees have a good work-life balance?

6. How does technology impact work-life balance?

7. What are some strategies for ensuring that you have enough leisure and rest time?

8. Do you think women face increasing pressure in today's society, compared to men?

9. Do you like working under pressure?

10. Do people need to give up work-life balance to get promotions and climb the corporate ladder?


**Writing Prompts**

1. Work-life balance is the responsibility of the employee. They should say no to overtime and working on vacation. Do you agree or disagree with this?

2. Women face too much pressure in today's society, with work and most of the responsibility for raising children. Do you agree with this?

# Before You Go

Thanks for using this book of conversation lessons. I hope that you've found it useful. If you liked the book, please consider leaving a review wherever you bought it. It'll help other teachers, like yourself, find this useful resource.

Also, be sure to check these out:

ESL Speaking (www.eslspeaking.org)

YouTube (www.youtube.com/c/jackiebolen)

Pinterest (www.pinterest.ca/eslspeaking)

Facebook (www.facebook.com/eslspeaking)

Get even more things ESL teaching, delivered straight to your inbox: (www.eslspeaking.org/subscribe).

Printed in Great Britain
by Amazon